How To Make Your Own Tin Foil Hat

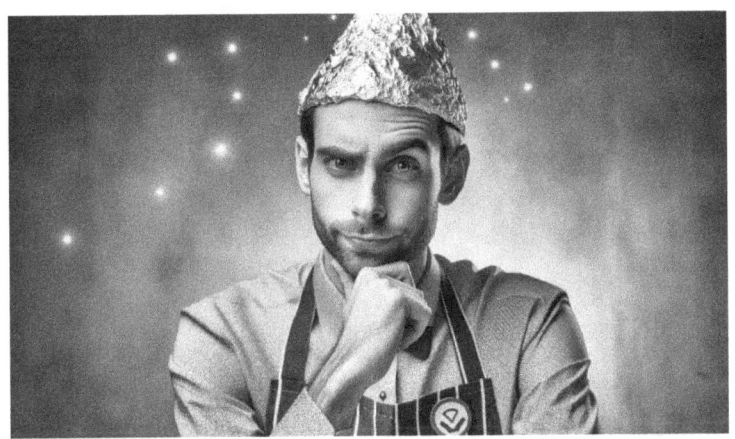

By Will Power

Key Takeaways

- Gather all the essential supplies for your homemade tin foil hat, because protection is key in style!
- Follow the simple, hilarious instructions to craft your very own tin foil hat and join the conspiracy fun.
- Customize your tin foil hat to suit your personality and enhance its effectiveness with these quirky tips.
- Explore expert-endorsed designs to elevate your tin foil hat game and shield yourself from those mind-reading aliens.
- Examine top conspiracy theories

This book seeks to provide you with everything you need to know about making your own tin foil hat and supplying you with a few conspiracy theories upon which you can hang your new hat.

Introduction to the World of Tin Foil Hats

Welcome to the peculiar and glittering world of tin foil hats, where practicality meets paranoia and fashion takes a shiny turn. Whether you're a seasoned conspiracy theorist or just someone looking to add a bit of sparkle to your headgear collection, this book is your ultimate guide to crafting the perfect tin foil hat.

But first, let's clear up a common misconception: tin foil hats aren't just for those who believe the government is beaming secret messages into their brains or that aliens are scanning their thoughts from orbit. No, dear reader, tin foil hats are for everyone! They are the universal symbol of questioning reality, protecting your thoughts, and, let's face it, having a bit of fun while doing it.

The Origins of Tin Foil Hats

The tin foil hat has a storied history, deeply embedded in both pop culture and the annals of paranoid folklore. The concept dates back to the early 20th century, notably appearing in science fiction literature. In 1927, Julian Huxley's short story "The Tissue-Culture King" presented the idea of tin foil headwear as a means to block telepathic communication. Since then, the tin foil hat has evolved from a literary device to a staple of conspiracy culture and, eventually, a tongue-in-cheek emblem of defiance against unseen forces.

Why Tin Foil?

You might be wondering, why tin foil? Why not lead, copper, or some other metal? Well, tin foil—more accurately, aluminum foil, as we use today—offers a perfect blend of flexibility, accessibility, and shiny aesthetics. It's available in almost every kitchen, easy to mold into various shapes, and reflective enough to catch the eye (or, as some claim, deflect those unwanted mind waves).

The Appeal of Tin Foil Hats

There's a certain charm to the tin foil hat. It represents more than just a barrier against potential mind control; it's a statement. It's about taking a stand against the invisible, the intangible, and sometimes, the improbable. It's about saying, "I control my own destiny, and I do it with style."

Moreover, the act of crafting a tin foil hat is a delightful blend of art and science. It's a DIY project that doesn't just occupy your hands but also engages your imagination. Whether you're sculpting a sleek, minimalist cap or an elaborate, multi-layered fortress, each hat is a unique creation, a personal shield against the unknown.

What You'll Find in This Book

In the pages that follow, we'll dive deep into the world of tin foil hats. We'll explore their history and the curious science behind them, break down the best materials and techniques for construction, and even touch on the fashion aspect—because why shouldn't your tin foil hat be both functional and fabulous?

Each chapter will guide you step-by-step through the process, from selecting the perfect foil to designing a hat that's not just protective but also a conversation starter. We'll also discuss how to reinforce your creations for those times when a single layer just isn't enough. By the end of this book, you'll be equipped with the knowledge and skills to make your own tin foil hat, tailored to your specific needs and style.

This guide is not just a step-by-step manual to craft your very own tin-foil hat—a must-have for every skeptic and free thinker, but also a dive into the quirky world of conspiracy theories.

Dive into the top 10 conspiracy theories that have fascinated and perplexed people for decades. From secret government mind control programs to hidden alien colonies, each theory is explored with a blend of skepticism and intrigue. Whether you're a believer or a curious skeptic, this book offers a lighthearted yet insightful look into the world of conspiracy theories

The Community

Crafting and wearing a tin foil hat can also be a communal activity. Join the ranks of fellow enthusiasts who embrace their hats as symbols of personal expression and playful skepticism. Share your designs, participate in tin foil hat meetups (yes, they exist), and become part of a unique subculture that values creativity and a healthy dose of skepticism.

So, grab a roll of tin foil, put on your thinking cap (literally), and prepare to embark on a journey of discovery, creativity, and a bit of tongue-in-cheek protection from those mysterious mind waves. Welcome to the world of tin foil hats!

The History of Tin Foil Hats:

From Sci-Fi to DIY

In the annals of headwear history, few items have as colorful and convoluted a story as the tin foil hat. This humble yet shiny creation has traveled from the pages of science fiction to the shelves of your local grocery store, becoming a symbol of both paranoia and playfulness.

Early Sci-Fi Roots

The concept of using metal to block telepathic communication first appeared in the realm of science fiction. In 1927, Julian Huxley's short story "The Tissue-Culture King" introduced readers to the idea that metal could shield one's thoughts from psychic invasion. While Huxley's tale didn't focus exclusively on tin foil hats, it set the stage for their eventual cultural emergence.

As the 20th century progressed, science fiction continued to explore themes of mind control and mental privacy. Stories about alien mind readers, government experiments, and secret devices to read and influence thoughts proliferated. In this fertile ground of speculative fiction, the notion of wearing a metal hat to guard against such intrusions took root.

Transition to Pop Culture

The leap from science fiction to popular culture was a natural one. As the Cold War heightened fears of espionage and brainwashing, the tin foil hat became a symbol of resistance against perceived threats. Films and television shows began to feature characters donning tin foil hats to protect themselves from mind control, further embedding the concept in the public consciousness.

One of the most notable moments in tin foil hat history came with the 1997 film "Signs," directed by M. Night Shyamalan. In the movie, a family uses tin foil hats to shield themselves from alien mind control, cementing the hat's place in pop culture as both a humorous and paranoid defense mechanism.

The Internet Era

With the advent of the internet, the tin foil hat found a new home. Online communities dedicated to conspiracy theories and alternative beliefs adopted the hat as a symbol of their skepticism and defiance. Memes and jokes about tin foil hats spread across forums and social media, blurring the lines between genuine belief and satire.

In this digital age, the tin foil hat has become more than just a physical object; it's a metaphor for questioning the status quo and guarding one's mental autonomy. It's a way to signal that you're not entirely on board with mainstream narratives, whether or not you actually believe in mind-reading technologies.

DIY Revolution

Today, making your own tin foil hat is a blend of art, science, and personal expression. The DIY movement has embraced tin foil hats, with enthusiasts sharing designs and tips for creating the most effective and stylish headgear. From simple caps to elaborate constructions that would make a Renaissance sculptor proud, tin foil hats are as diverse as their makers.

This chapter will delve into the historical journey of the tin foil hat, exploring its origins in science fiction, its rise in popular culture, and its current status as a symbol of DIY ingenuity and skeptical humor. We'll look at key moments and figures that have shaped the tin foil hat's legacy and discuss how it has become a staple of both conspiracy culture and creative crafting.

Tin Foil Hat in Pop Culture

Tin foil hats have made their mark in various forms of media, from movies to music. Understanding their role in pop culture can deepen your appreciation for this quirky accessory:

1. **Movies and TV Shows:** Films like "Signs" and shows like "The X-Files" have featured characters using tin foil hats to protect themselves from aliens and government conspiracies. These depictions have cemented the hat's place as a symbol of paranoia and defiance.
2. **Music and Art:** Musicians and artists often use tin foil hats as metaphors for societal skepticism and individuality. They appear in album covers, music videos, and artworks that explore themes of control and freedom.
3. **Literature:** Books and comics sometimes feature characters who don tin foil hats, either as a protective measure or as a symbol of their unique perspective on the world. These stories highlight the hat's dual role as both a shield and a statement.

Gathering the Necessary Materials

for your DIY Tin Foil Hat

To create your own tin foil hat, there are several essential items you'll need to assemble. First, grab an aluminum foil roll, construction paper, glue, and foam mannequin head from home, school, or a friend. You may also require work gloves, cricut blades, and a dome to shape your hat effectively. When selecting high-quality tin foil for your hat, make sure it's sturdy and will maintain its shape. Consider researching sources like wikihow or articles from reputable sites for tips on How To Make your Own Tin Foil Hat. Finding the right materials is the first step in constructing a tinfoil hat that fits comfortably and serves its purpose.

- Don't forget to check your local conspiracy theory forums for DIY tin foil hat making hacks!
-
- Remember, the shinier the tin foil, the better it will protect you from mind control!
-
- If you run out of aluminum foil, improvise with household items like potato chip bags or soda cans.
-
- For added flair, consider decorating your tin foil hat with stickers or glitter.
-
- Make sure to measure your head circumference accurately to avoid any aluminum foil mishaps.

Essential Items to Assemble

When embarking on the endeavor of How To Make your Own Tin Foil Hat, there are several essential items you will need to assemble. A roll of high-quality tin foil will be the cornerstone of your project. Additionally, having a sturdy bottle or radio antennae to use as a mold for shaping your hat will prove to be beneficial. Ensuring you have a pair of scissors to cut the tin foil sheets to size is crucial for precision. For added customization, keeping a kitchen torch handy can assist in making fixes or modifications to your creation. To further enhance your experience, consider gathering product recommendations for tin foil from reputable sources like wikihow newsletter or YouTube tutorials for valuable tips and tricks.

In order to create the perfect tin foil hat, having the right materials is key. You will need a large sheet of tin foil to serve as the base of your hat. Utilizing a corner piece to fashion the brim and mold the tin foil into a diamond shape will give your hat a unique touch. For those looking to personalize their tin foil hat further, incorporating bits and pieces such as airpods or small illustrations can add a fun and quirky element. Remember to always respect copyright laws when using images or logos on your hat – it's essential to obtain consent if needed. By following these guidelines and gathering the necessary items, you'll be well on your way to creating a novel and stylish accessory for your How To Make your Own Tin Foil Hat venture.

Selecting High Quality Tin Foil for Your Hat

When it comes to selecting high-quality tin foil for your DIY tin foil hat, it's crucial to consider the durability and thickness of the foil. Opt for tin foil that is sturdy enough to hold its shape when crafting your hat. Look for reputable brands or shops that offer quality aluminum foil, ensuring that it will effectively block any unwanted communication signals. Additionally, make sure the foil is free from wrinkles or tears to achieve a sleek and polished finish for your hat. Check out resources like iStock or sunshine review for recommendations on where to purchase top-grade foil for your How To Make your Own Tin Foil Hat project.

For superior results in creating your tin foil hat, choose aluminum foil that is easy to mold and manipulate. The flexibility of the foil will make it easier to craft intricate designs or shapes for your hat, whether you're going for a classic look or a more avant-garde style. To prevent any skin irritation, opt for foil that is smooth and free from sharp edges or corners. Consider experimenting with different textures or finishes for a unique touch to your hat. Remember, the right choice of tin foil can make all the difference in the end product of your How To Make your Own Tin Foil Hat masterpiece.

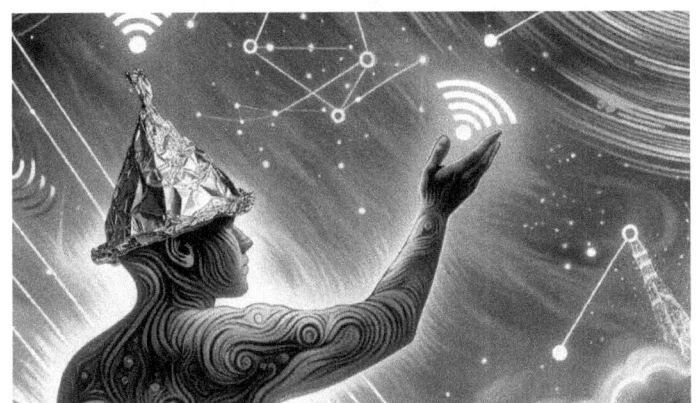

Step by Step Instruction to Create Your Tin Foil Hat

When it comes to How To Make your Own Tin Foil Hat, the first step is gathering all the necessary materials. Before starting the craft, make sure you have a good quality tin foil, especially if you want to create a hat that will last. Think about the purpose of your hat too; whether it's for a fun costume like a tin man costume, for some sports activities, or simply as a privacy policy statement. Once you've got your materials laid out, you can proceed with preparing your tin foil sheets by cutting them in a rectangle shape. The next part involves assembling and molding your hat, which can be a fun and creative process. By following these simple steps, you can have a stylish tin foil hat ready to wear in no time.

Preparing Your Tin Foil Sheets

To prepare your tin foil sheets for crafting your tin foil hat, start by laying out a large sheet of aluminum foil on a table. Gently fold the foil in half to create a crease down the middle, allowing you to easily cut and shape it for your hat. Use a pair of scissors to cut the foil, ensuring you have enough material to cover the desired hat size. If you prefer a stiffer hat that holds its shape well, consider applying a light layer of starch to the foil before molding it. Let your imagination run wild as you craft your personalized headpiece – from adding pompoms and jewels for a touch of flair to creating an alfalfa twist for a whimsical and unique look. Experiment with different folding techniques and shapes to make your tin foil hat truly stand out amongst the rest. How To Make your Own Tin Foil Hat just got more exciting and dynamic with these creative tips!

Assembling and Molding Your Hat

To assemble and mold your tin foil hat, start by cutting out an oval shape from your hat foil large enough to fit your head comfortably. You can use scissors for this step, ensuring the size is just right for a snug yet comfortable fit. Once you have your oval piece, carefully mold it around a bowl or other object that closely resembles the shape of your head. Gently press and shape the foil to create the desired hat form. This method ensures a personalized fit and is a crucial step in the How To Make your Own Tin Foil Hat process. For added flair, consider adding embellishments like glitter, sequins, or even small styrofoam skulls to your hat for a unique touch that sets your creation apart from others.

When molding your tin foil hat, you can also experiment with various possibilities to customize its appearance. For inspiration, check out videos featuring different tin foil hat designs online or research sources that offer unique hat foil crafting ideas. By exploring a variety of examples and expert-approved tin foil hat designs, you can enhance your crafting experience and create a hat foil masterpiece that truly reflects your style. Don't hesitate to get creative and think outside the box - perhaps you want to incorporate elements from your favorite hobbies, such as a tiny wine glass for wine lovers or tiny garden tools for those with a green thumb. The key is to have fun with the process and let your imagination run wild as you craft your very own tin foil hat masterpiece.

Tips to Customize and Improve Your Tin Foil Hat

When it comes to customizing and improving your tin foil hat, the key is to get creative with your materials and make it unique to your style. Incorporate different colors of tin foil or even mix materials like vinyl plank for a modern twist. Enhancing the comfort and fit of your hat can be easily achieved by adding padding inside or adjusting the rim to better suit your head shape. Additionally, getting inspired by famous tin foil hat wearers and their designs can help you adopt techniques to elevate your own creation. By following these tips, you can personalize your tin foil hat and stand out in the world of DIY headwear.

If you are delving into the realm of How To Make your Own Tin Foil Hat, why not infuse some creativity into your materials selection? Think beyond the standard tin foil box and explore unconventional items like rubber bands, starbucks cups, or even particle board advertisements. Consider incorporating elements that resonate with you personally, whether it's adding a whimsical touch for the kids with animal shapes or embracing a more sophisticated vibe by crafting a hat that mimics the curve of a whalebone media logo. The key is to let your imagination run wild and see how these diverse materials can breathe new life into your tin foil creation.

When you open up the floodgates of creativity in your tin foil hat project, the possibilities are endless. Experiment with innovative ways to mold and shape your hat, be it by creating a funnel shape for a futuristic look or adding smallurl accents for a touch of flair. Harness the power of love for breast cancer awareness by incorporating pink tin foil accents, or concoct a hat that doubles as a time capsule by hiding cookies or favorite recipes inside. Your tin foil hat isn't just a mere head accessory – it's a canvas for self-expression and a beacon of ingenuity in a sea of mundane headpieces.

Enhancing Comfort and Fit through Modifications

To enhance the comfort and fit of your tin foil hat, consider making adjustments for a more personalized feel. Start by molding the hat on a mannequin or a similar object to create the desired shape. Pay attention to the edges and corners to ensure a snug fit that is comfortable to wear for extended periods. You can also add small modifications like using pieces of whalebone or flexible materials to reinforce certain areas of the hat, especially if it's intended for children. By customizing the fit of your tin foil hat, you can optimize its comfort level and wear it with confidence in various settings, whether at work or during social gatherings such as baby showers or parties.

Material	Color	Additional Tips
Tin Foil	Silver, Gold, Red, Blue	Experiment with crinkling techniques for texture
Vinyl Plank	Black, White, Metallic	Combine with tin foil for a futuristic look
Padding	Any color	Use memory foam for maximum comfort
Rim Adjustment	N/A	Customize the shape to fit your head perfectly

Fashion Forward:

Designing Tin Foil Hats That Turn Heads

Who says protection can't be stylish? In this chapter, we'll explore the art of designing tin foil hats that not only shield your thoughts but also make a bold fashion statement. From minimalist designs to avant-garde creations, we'll cover a range of styles and provide tips on how to craft a hat that's as chic as it is functional.

Expert Approved Tin Foil Hat Designs

When it comes to designing your tin foil hat, the possibilities are endless. By exploring different categories like arts and crafts, you can draw inspiration from a variety of sources to create a hat that truly stands out. From tinfoil cowboy hats to intricate designs adorned with sequins, the options to personalize your foil hat are abundant. Take a cue from famous tin foil hat wearers on how to make your own tin foil hat uniquely yours. Whether you prefer a classic look or want to push the boundaries with a bold statement piece, this info-packed page will guide you through the creative process. So, roll up your sleeves, grab some tinfoil, and let your imagination flow as you embark on this exciting DIY project.

Minimalist Chic

For those who prefer a subtle approach, minimalist tin foil hats offer protection without drawing too much attention. These designs focus on clean lines, simple shapes, and functionality.

1. **The Classic Cap:** A straightforward design that covers the top of your head and extends just past the ears. Easy to make and wear, the classic cap is perfect for everyday use.
2. **The Headband Style:** A more discreet option, this design involves wrapping a strip of tin foil around your forehead and securing it at the back. It provides a basic level of protection while remaining low-profile.
3. **The Skullcap:** Similar to the classic cap but with a snug fit that contours to your head. This design is sleek and practical, offering good coverage with minimal bulk.

Bold and Daring

For those who want their tin foil hat to stand out, bold designs incorporate unique shapes, embellishments, and creative touches that make a statement.

1. **The Crown:** Why not feel like royalty while blocking those signals? A crown-shaped tin foil hat, complete with peaks and points, adds a regal flair to your protective gear.
2. **The Mohawk:** Channel your inner rebel with a mohawk-style tin foil hat. This design features a strip of spiky foil running from the front to the back of your head, giving you an edgy look.
3. **The Sculptural Masterpiece:** For the truly artistic, sculptural hats take tin foil to new heights. Create elaborate shapes and forms, from spirals and swirls to geometric patterns, that showcase your creativity.

Functional and Practical

If you're looking for a design that combines style with additional functionality, these options offer practical features that go beyond simple protection.

1. **The Visor:** Adding a visor to your tin foil hat can help shield your eyes from bright lights or provide a bit of shade. It's a practical addition that enhances both comfort and style.
2. **The Earflap Hat:** For colder climates or those who want extra coverage, a hat with earflaps provides additional protection and warmth. Secure the flaps under your chin for a snug fit.
3. **The Multi-Layer Fortress:** When one layer isn't enough, go for a multi-layer design that offers maximum shielding. This hat features multiple overlapping layers of foil, ensuring top-notch protection from all angles.

Tips for Crafting Stylish Tin Foil Hats

1. **Experiment with Shapes:** Don't be afraid to try out different shapes and styles. Use household items like bowls or balloons to help mold the foil into unique forms.
2. **Add Embellishments:** Decorate your hat with stickers, paint, or other materials to personalize your design. Just make sure any additions don't compromise the hat's protective properties.
3. **Combine Materials:** Mix tin foil with other materials, such as fabric or cardboard, to add structure and variety to your design. This can also help improve the hat's comfort and fit.
4. **Consider Comfort:** Make sure your hat is comfortable to wear. Line the inside with a soft material or adjust the fit to prevent it from being too tight or loose.
5. **Test and Refine:** Wear your hat around the house to test its fit and functionality. Make any necessary adjustments to ensure it stays in place and provides the desired level of protection.

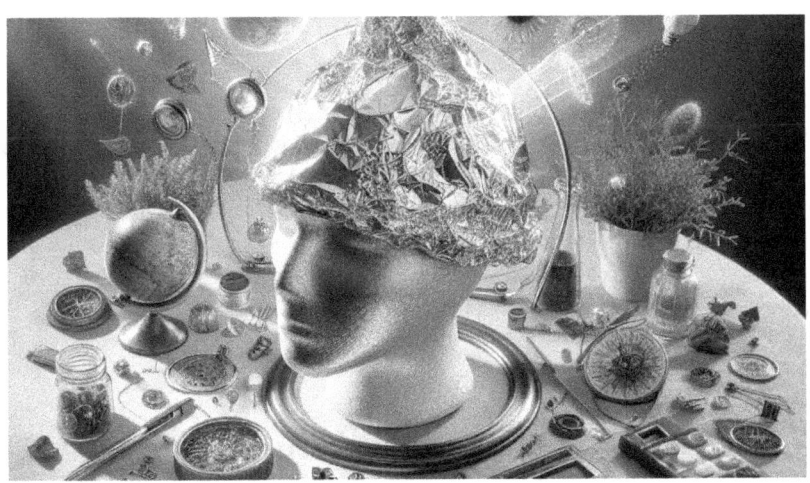

Unusual Tin Foil Hat Styles for Inspiration

For those looking to go beyond the traditional tin foil hat style, there are numerous unusual designs that can inspire your creativity. Experiment with shapes, sizes, and accessories to customize your tin foil hat. Consider crafting a cowboy hat-inspired tin foil hat for a whimsical touch or creating a futuristic helmet using aluminum pieces for a unique look. By incorporating different elements in your design, you can elevate your tin foil hat game and stand out from the crowd. Whether you are seeking a fun twist on the classic tin foil hat or aiming to make a statement with your headwear, exploring unconventional styles can add an element of excitement to your DIY project. So, let your imagination run wild and craft a tin foil hat that reflects your personality and style while keeping you protected from the glare of unwanted signals.

Adopting Techniques from Famous Tin Foil Hat Wearers

If you want to adopt the techniques from famous tin foil hat wearers, start by exploring the wide variety of creative hat designs showcased by individuals like Patrick, a pioneer in tin foil hat fashion. To enhance the accuracy and research source of your hat-making process, visit www.wikihow.com for step-by-step instructions on How To Make your Own Tin Foil Hat. By incorporating aspects from renowned hat styles, you can elevate your hat's appearance and functionality, adding unique sections and embellishments such as tin foil boat hat downloads or alien abduction motifs.

When delving into the world of famous tin foil hat wearers, consider the craftsmanship behind iconic designs like cowboy hats or futuristic space helmets. Use aluminum foil to construct your hat material and opt for quality scissors to ensure precise cutting and styling. Experiment with different decorations such as crop circles or whalebone accents for a whimsical touch. By following expert suggestions and reviewing tin foil hat techniques on platforms like Facebook or Pinterest, you can tailor your hat to suit your preferences and reflect your personality.

Conclusion

Expert-Approved Tin Foil Hat Designs include Unusual Tin Foil Hat Styles for Inspiration and Adopting Techniques from Famous Tin Foil Hat Wearers. These designs guide you on How To Make your Own Tin Foil Hat. The article outlines Step-by-Step Instruction to Create Your Tin Foil Hat, from Preparing Your Tin Foil Sheets to Assembling and Molding Your Hat, ensuring you have Essential Items to Assemble. Tips to Customize and Improve Your Tin Foil Hat offer ways to get creative with your materials and enhance comfort and fit through modifications. Whether you choose to don a classic tin foil hat or experiment with unique styles, these hacks provide personalized options for your How To Make your Own Tin Foil Hat journey.

The Science Behind the Shine:

How Tin Foil Blocks Those Pesky Signals

At the heart of the tin foil hat's appeal is its supposed ability to block or deflect various types of signals. But how does a thin sheet of metal accomplish this? In this chapter, we'll dive into the science behind tin foil and explore how it interacts with electromagnetic waves, radio frequencies, and other potential mind-meddling signals.

Electromagnetic Shielding

Electromagnetic shielding is the process of blocking or attenuating electromagnetic fields using a barrier made of conductive material. Tin foil, being a good conductor of electricity, can act as such a barrier, reflecting and absorbing electromagnetic waves.

1. **Reflection:** Tin foil's shiny surface reflects electromagnetic waves, preventing them from passing through. This is similar to how a mirror reflects light, bouncing the waves away from the surface.
2. **Absorption:** Some of the waves are absorbed by the foil, converting their energy into small amounts of heat. This absorption further reduces the intensity of the waves that might reach your brain.

Blocking Radio Frequencies

Radio frequencies (RF) are a subset of electromagnetic waves used for communication signals, including radio broadcasts, cell phone transmissions, and Wi-Fi. Tin foil can block these frequencies by creating a Faraday cage effect.

1. **Faraday Cage Principle:** A Faraday cage is an enclosure made of conductive material that blocks external electric fields. When electromagnetic waves encounter the tin foil, the electrons in the foil rearrange themselves to counteract the external field, effectively canceling it out within the enclosed space (your head).
2. **Attenuation Levels:** The effectiveness of the foil in blocking RF signals depends on its thickness, the frequency of the waves, and the completeness of the coverage. Higher frequencies require more robust shielding, which is why heavy-duty foil or multiple layers might be more effective.

Myth vs. Reality

While the science of electromagnetic shielding is real, the effectiveness of a tin foil hat in practical scenarios is a subject of debate and humor. Here are a few points to consider:

1. **Partial Shielding:** A tin foil hat might block some signals, but because it doesn't completely enclose the head like a true Faraday cage, its shielding effectiveness is limited. The open bottom allows for some signals to penetrate.
2. **Signal Enhancement:** Interestingly, some studies have suggested that certain designs of tin foil hats could actually amplify signals rather than block them, depending on the frequency and shape of the hat.
3. **Psychological Comfort:** Beyond the physical effects, wearing a tin foil hat can provide psychological comfort, giving the wearer a sense of control and protection against perceived threats, even if the actual effectiveness is limited.

Practical Applications

Understanding the science behind tin foil and electromagnetic shielding can help you design a more effective hat. Here are some practical tips:

1. **Complete Coverage:** Aim for a design that covers as much of your head as possible to maximize the shielding effect. Consider adding a chin strap or neck guard to reduce the open areas.
2. **Layering for Protection:** Multiple layers of foil can enhance the shielding effect, especially against higher frequency signals. Experiment with different configurations to find the most effective setup.
3. **Reflective Surfaces:** Ensure that the shiny side of the foil is facing outward, as this maximizes the reflective properties and improves the hat's ability to deflect incoming waves.
4. **Testing and Tweaking:** Use simple devices like a radio or cell phone to test the effectiveness of your hat. If signals are noticeably weaker, you've likely created a decent shield.

Advanced Techniques:

Reinforcing Your Tin Foil Hat for Ultimate Defense

For those who want to take their tin foil hat to the next level, this chapter covers advanced techniques for reinforcing and enhancing your hat's protective capabilities. We'll explore methods to add strength, improve durability, and maximize shielding, ensuring your hat is ready for anything.

Multi-Layer Construction

One of the simplest ways to enhance your tin foil hat's effectiveness is by adding multiple layers. Each additional layer provides extra protection and helps to block a wider range of frequencies.

1. **Layering for Strength:** Start with a basic hat shape and add multiple layers of foil, pressing each layer firmly to remove air pockets. This technique not only increases shielding but also makes the hat more durable.
2. **Alternating Materials:** For even better protection, consider alternating layers of tin foil with other materials like fabric or plastic. This creates a composite structure that can block a wider range of signals.
3. **Reinforced Edges:** Pay special attention to the edges of your hat, which can be points of weakness. Reinforce them with extra layers or fold the foil over several times to create a thicker barrier.

Structural Enhancements

To ensure your hat maintains its shape and provides consistent protection, consider adding structural elements that enhance stability and coverage.

1. **Foil Tape Reinforcement:** Use foil tape to secure seams and add rigidity to your hat. This is particularly useful for more complex designs that need extra support.
2. **Wire Framework:** Incorporate a lightweight wire framework into your hat's design. Bend the wire into the desired shape and cover it with foil, creating a sturdy and flexible structure.
3. **Cardboard Supports:** For larger or more elaborate hats, use cardboard to create internal supports. This helps maintain the hat's shape and provides a solid base for the foil layers.

Enhancing Coverage

Maximizing the coverage area of your hat can improve its effectiveness in blocking signals. Consider extending the coverage beyond just the top of your head.

1. **Neck and Shoulder Shields:** Extend the foil down to cover your neck and shoulders, creating a more comprehensive shield. Attach the extended sections securely to the main hat to prevent gaps.
2. **Face Guard:** Add a front flap or visor that extends over your face, providing extra protection for your eyes and forehead. This can also help reduce glare from bright lights.
3. **Full Head Enclosure:** For maximum coverage, design a hat that completely encloses your head, similar to a hood. Ensure there are ventilation holes to prevent overheating.

Testing and Adjusting

Once you've reinforced your hat, it's important to test its effectiveness and make any necessary adjustments to improve performance.

1. **Signal Testing:** Use a simple radio or mobile device to test the hat's ability to block signals. Experiment with different frequencies and positions to see how well your hat performs.
2. **Comfort and Fit:** Wear the hat for extended periods to ensure it remains comfortable and secure. Make adjustments to the fit or add padding if needed.
3. **Durability Check:** Put your hat through its paces by bending, folding, and wearing it in different conditions. This helps identify any weak spots or areas that need additional reinforcement.

The Tin Foil Hat Lifestyle:

Embracing the Shield and the Style

Wearing a tin foil hat is more than just a quirky fashion statement; it's a lifestyle choice that reflects a unique blend of humor, skepticism, and personal expression. In this final chapter, we'll explore how to incorporate your tin foil hat into your daily life and connect with a community of like-minded individuals who share your passion for shiny headgear.

Everyday Wear and Practical Tips

Integrating a tin foil hat into your daily routine can be both fun and functional. Here's how to make the most of your headgear:

1. **Casual Outings:** Wear your hat during casual outings, like trips to the grocery store or walks in the park. It's a great conversation starter and a way to spread a little joy and curiosity.
2. **Special Events:** Make your tin foil hat the highlight of parties, gatherings, and themed events. Whether it's a costume party or a casual get-together, your hat will be the talk of the town.
3. **Daily Protection:** If you genuinely believe in the protective powers of your hat, incorporate it into your daily routine. Wear it while working from home, watching TV, or even sleeping to ensure you're always shielded.
4. **Practical Adjustments:** To make your hat more practical, consider adding features like a removable lining for easy cleaning or a foldable design for convenient storage.

Community and Connection

The tin foil hat community is a vibrant and welcoming group that celebrates creativity, individuality, and a healthy dose of skepticism. Here's how to connect and engage with fellow enthusiasts:

1. **Online Forums and Groups:** Join online communities dedicated to tin foil hats and related topics. Share your designs, exchange tips, and participate in discussions about the latest trends and theories.
2. **Meetups and Events:** Attend or organize local meetups and events where tin foil hat enthusiasts can gather to showcase their creations and share their experiences. From informal gatherings to themed parties, these events are a great way to connect in person.
3. **Social Media Sharing:** Use social media platforms to share photos and stories about your tin foil hat adventures. Hashtags like #TinFoilHat and #ShinyStyle can help you find and connect with others who appreciate the art of reflective headwear.
4. **Collaborative Projects:** Collaborate with fellow crafters and enthusiasts on projects like group designs or community challenges. Working together can spark new ideas and create lasting friendships.

Embracing the Fun and Humor

At its core, the tin foil hat lifestyle is about having fun and embracing a playful approach to life's mysteries. Here's how to keep the spirit of humor and creativity alive:

1. **Celebrate the Quirky:** Embrace the quirky and unconventional aspects of wearing a tin foil hat. Whether it's the puzzled looks you get from strangers or the chuckles from friends, enjoy the lightheartedness it brings.
2. **Stay Curious:** Keep your curiosity alive by exploring new designs, materials, and theories. The world of tin foil hats is ever-evolving, and there's always something new to discover.
3. **Spread the Joy:** Share the joy of tin foil hats with others. Gift a handmade hat to a friend, host a tin foil hat crafting session, or simply wear your hat with pride and a smile.
4. **Balance Skepticism with Positivity:** While tin foil hats can symbolize skepticism, remember to balance it with positivity and open-mindedness. Use your hat as a reminder to question, but also to celebrate the fun and wonder in life.

Exploring New Horizons with Tin Foil Hats

Embracing the tin foil hat lifestyle doesn't have to be confined to the confines of everyday wear or social gatherings. Here are some creative and out-of-the-box ways to expand your horizons with tin foil hats:

1. **Tin Foil Hat Competitions:** Participate in or host competitions where enthusiasts showcase their most inventive and stylish hats. Categories could include "Most Creative Design," "Best Use of Materials," or "Most Practical Hat." Winners can take home the coveted title of "Tin Foil Hat Champion."
2. **Crafting Workshops:** Offer or attend workshops focused on the art of making tin foil hats. These workshops can teach basic crafting skills, advanced techniques, and the science behind electromagnetic shielding. They are a fantastic way to learn, create, and meet new friends.
3. **Educational Outreach:** Use tin foil hats as a fun tool for educational outreach. Teach kids about the science of electromagnetic waves, the history of protective gear, or the importance of questioning and critical thinking. The hats provide a memorable and engaging way to learn complex concepts.
4. **Charity and Awareness Campaigns:** Leverage the attention-grabbing nature of tin foil hats to raise awareness for causes you care about. Whether it's environmental protection, mental health, or technological literacy, your shiny headgear can draw attention and spark conversations.

Now let us look into the world of conspiracies

In an age where information is at our fingertips, the allure of conspiracy theories remains as potent as ever. These narratives, often shrouded in mystery and intrigue, captivate our imagination and challenge our understanding of the world. From whispers of secret societies to grandiose tales of government cover-ups, conspiracy theories have woven themselves into the fabric of our culture.

But what drives people to believe in these often outlandish claims? Why do some of these theories persist despite overwhelming evidence to the contrary? This book delves into the top eleven conspiracy theories that have captured the public's attention, exploring their origins, the evidence that fuels them, and the impact they have on society.

The Psychology Behind Conspiracy Theories

Conspiracy theories often thrive in times of uncertainty and change. They offer simple explanations for complex problems, providing a sense of control and understanding when reality feels chaotic. People turn to these theories for various reasons, including:

1. **A Need for Understanding:** In a world full of chaos, conspiracy theories offer seemingly clear and definitive answers.
2. **Mistrust of Authority:** A deep-seated skepticism towards government and institutions fuels belief in these theories.
3. **A Sense of Community:** Believers often find solace in communities that share their views, creating a bond over common beliefs.
4. **Cognitive Biases:** Human psychology is prone to patterns, and we often see connections where none exist, leading us to believe in elaborate conspiracies.

The Evolution of Conspiracy Theories

Throughout history, conspiracy theories have evolved, adapting to the times and technological advancements. From medieval tales of witchcraft to modern theories about space travel and digital surveillance, these stories morph to fit the cultural and societal context of their era. With the advent of the internet, the spread of these theories has accelerated, allowing them to reach a global audience almost instantaneously.

The Role of Media

The media plays a crucial role in both the spread and debunking of conspiracy theories. Sensationalist reporting can amplify these stories, giving them credibility and reach. Social media platforms, in particular, have become breeding grounds for conspiracy theories, where algorithms favor engaging content, often pushing these narratives to the forefront. Conversely, reputable news outlets and fact-checkers work tirelessly to debunk these myths, presenting evidence-based counterarguments.

The Impact on Society

Belief in conspiracy theories can have profound effects on society. While some theories are harmless, providing nothing more than entertainment or fodder for discussion, others can lead to dangerous consequences. Misinformation can erode trust in public institutions, influence political processes, and even incite violence. Understanding the mechanics behind these beliefs is crucial in addressing the challenges they pose.

Why These Thirteen?

The thirteen conspiracy theories selected for this book represent a broad spectrum of beliefs, from the historically significant to the bizarrely contemporary. Each chapter delves into the origins of these theories, the evidence (or lack thereof) supporting them, and their cultural impact. By examining these stories, we can better understand the human propensity for believing in the extraordinary.

Whether you are a skeptic looking to understand the allure of conspiracy theories or a believer seeking validation, this book aims to provide a comprehensive overview of some of the most intriguing and enduring conspiracy theories of our time.

1: The Moon Landing Hoax

In 1969, the world watched in awe as NASA's Apollo 11 mission successfully landed humans on the moon for the first time. Yet, almost immediately, skeptics began to question the authenticity of this monumental achievement. The Moon Landing Hoax theory posits that the Apollo missions were elaborate fabrications, staged by NASA and the U.S. government to win the Space Race against the Soviet Union.

The Origins of the Theory

The Moon Landing Hoax theory gained traction in the 1970s, primarily due to the work of Bill Kaysing, a former U.S. Navy officer and technical writer at Rocketdyne, a company involved in the Apollo program. In his 1974 book "We Never Went to the Moon: America's Thirty Billion Dollar Swindle," Kaysing argued that the technology required for the Apollo missions was far beyond what was available at the time and that the landings were staged on Earth.

Kaysing's arguments, coupled with the era's distrust in government following events like the Vietnam War and the Watergate scandal, found a receptive audience. Over time, various proponents have added their claims and interpretations, creating a complex web of assertions supporting the hoax theory.

Key Arguments and Counterarguments

1. **The Van Allen Radiation Belts**
   - **Claim:** The Apollo missions could not have passed through the Van Allen radiation belts without exposing astronauts to lethal doses of radiation.
   - **Counter:** NASA and independent scientists have explained that the Apollo spacecraft's trajectory and speed minimized exposure, and the craft's shielding provided adequate protection.
2. **No Stars in the Lunar Photos**
   - **Claim:** The absence of stars in the photographs taken on the moon's surface suggests that the images were taken in a studio, where stars were omitted to avoid revealing their true location.
   - **Counter:** Professional photographers and imaging experts explain that the camera settings used to capture the bright lunar surface would not have picked up the much dimmer stars in the background.
3. **The Waving Flag**
   - **Claim:** The American flag appears to wave in the wind in videos from the moon, which is impossible in the vacuum of space.
   - **Counter:** The flag's movement is attributed to its being manipulated by the astronauts during setup. The flag had a horizontal rod along its top to keep it extended, and the slight motion was a result of inertia in the vacuum.
4. **Unexplained Shadows**

- Claim: Shadows in the lunar photos are inconsistent with a single light source, suggesting multiple light sources, as would be found in a studio.
- Counter: Photographers and scientists point out that the uneven lunar surface and the reflection of light off the moon's surface can create the appearance of multiple light sources.

5. **The Technology Argument**
   - Claim: The technology of the 1960s was not advanced enough to safely land humans on the moon and return them to Earth.
   - Counter: This argument overlooks the extensive testing, research, and engineering advancements made by NASA in the years leading up to the Apollo missions. The Saturn V rocket and the Lunar Module were both state-of-the-art, having undergone rigorous development and testing.

Cultural Impact

The Moon Landing Hoax theory has had a significant impact on popular culture. It has been referenced in movies, TV shows, and literature, often as a metaphor for skepticism and distrust in authority. The theory has also persisted despite numerous debunkings by experts and evidence from subsequent lunar missions, including those by other countries and private entities.

The Reality

Decades of evidence, including samples brought back from the moon, data from later missions, and independent verification from other countries' space programs, support the fact that the Apollo moon landings were genuine. However, the Moon Landing Hoax theory remains a compelling example of how conspiracy theories can take root and persist, fueled by a combination of skepticism, mistrust, and a desire to question the official narrative.

2: 9/11: The Inside Job

September 11, 2001, remains one of the most significant and tragic days in modern history. The terrorist attacks on the World Trade Center and the Pentagon shook the world and changed the course of history. Yet, almost immediately after the attacks, theories emerged suggesting that the U.S. government or other shadowy entities were involved in orchestrating or allowing the attacks to happen as part of a larger agenda.

The Origins of the Theory

The "9/11 Truth" movement argues that the official account of the attacks is either incomplete or intentionally misleading. This movement gained momentum in the early 2000s, driven by questions about the collapse of the Twin Towers and Building 7, the attack on the Pentagon, and the response of U.S. military and intelligence agencies.

Key figures in the movement, such as architect Richard Gage and filmmaker Michael Moore, have argued that the events of 9/11 could not have occurred as described in the official narrative. They claim that the attacks were either facilitated or orchestrated by elements within the U.S. government as a pretext for expanding military actions and curtailing civil liberties.

Key Arguments and Counterarguments

1. **Controlled Demolition of the Twin Towers**
   - **Claim:** The collapse of the Twin Towers and Building 7 exhibited characteristics of a controlled demolition, such as free-fall acceleration and the symmetrical fall of the buildings.
   - **Counter:** Structural engineers and experts have explained that the intense heat from the jet fuel and subsequent fires weakened the steel framework of the buildings, leading to their collapse. The collapse of Building 7 was also attributed to fire damage and structural failure.
2. **The Pentagon Attack**
   - **Claim:** Some theorists argue that a missile, not a commercial airliner, hit the Pentagon, citing the relatively small size of the impact hole and the limited amount of visible debris.
   - **Counter:** Numerous eyewitnesses saw American Airlines Flight 77 crash into the Pentagon, and wreckage consistent with a Boeing 757 was recovered at the site. The damage was also consistent with an aircraft impact.
3. **Foreknowledge and Inaction**
   - **Claim:** There are assertions that key individuals or agencies within the U.S. government had foreknowledge of the attacks and either did nothing to prevent them or actively facilitated them.
   - **Counter:** Investigations, including the 9/11 Commission Report, have acknowledged failures in intelligence and communication but found no evidence of active facilitation or intentional inaction by U.S. officials.

4. **Financial Gains**
   - **Claim:** Unusual stock market activity, such as put options on airline stocks, suggests foreknowledge of the attacks for financial gain.
   - **Counter:** Investigations into these trades found no evidence of foreknowledge or illicit financial gains related to the 9/11 attacks.

Cultural Impact

The 9/11 Inside Job theory has had a profound impact on public discourse and has been the subject of numerous documentaries, books, and online discussions. It reflects a deep-seated mistrust in government and the mainstream media and highlights the power of conspiracy theories to shape public perception of significant events.

The Reality

Extensive investigations, including the 9/11 Commission Report and independent studies, have thoroughly examined the events of 9/11. While acknowledging failures in intelligence and response, these investigations have found no credible evidence supporting the claims of a controlled demolition or intentional facilitation of the attacks by the U.S. government. The 9/11 attacks were a complex and unprecedented event carried out by the terrorist group al-Qaeda, as detailed in numerous credible sources.

3: The Illuminati: Control Behind the Scenes

The Illuminati, often depicted as a shadowy and all-powerful organization, is said to control world events from behind the scenes. This theory suggests that a secret society of elites manipulates governments, economies, and societies to achieve a New World Order.

The Origins of the Theory

The modern concept of the Illuminati has roots in historical fact. The original Illuminati was a Bavarian secret society founded in 1776 by Adam Weishaupt. Its goals were to promote Enlightenment ideals and to oppose religious and state oppression. The Bavarian government banned the Illuminati in 1785, and it was disbanded.

However, the idea of the Illuminati persisted and evolved. In the 19th and 20th centuries, various writers and conspiracy theorists began to link the Illuminati to other secret societies and alleged plots. This modern version of the Illuminati is often portrayed as a global cabal seeking to establish a totalitarian world government.

Key Arguments and Counterarguments

1. **Symbolism and Influence**
   - **Claim:** The Illuminati uses symbols such as the all-seeing eye and the pyramid to mark their influence on global events and institutions.
   - **Counter:** Many symbols attributed to the Illuminati have other historical and cultural meanings. The all-seeing eye, for example, is also a symbol used in various religious and artistic contexts.
2. **Control of Governments and Corporations**
   - **Claim:** The Illuminati manipulates world events and controls governments and major corporations to achieve their goals.
   - **Counter:** While powerful individuals and groups do exert significant influence over global affairs, there is no concrete evidence of a single, all-powerful organization orchestrating these events.
3. **Cultural and Media Presence**
   - **Claim:** The entertainment industry is allegedly filled with Illuminati symbolism, and celebrities are purported to be members or pawns of the Illuminati.
   - **Counter:** Pop culture often appropriates and repurposes symbols for artistic expression and intrigue. The presence of these symbols in media is more likely due to their mysterious and captivating nature rather than actual control by a secret society.
4. **New World Order**
   - **Claim:** The ultimate goal of the Illuminati is to establish a New World Order, a single authoritarian world government.
   - **Counter:** While the concept of a New World Order is a common theme in conspiracy theories, there is no substantive evidence linking this idea to the Illuminati or any real-world plan to establish such a government.

Cultural Impact

The Illuminati conspiracy theory has become a staple of popular culture, appearing in films, books, music, and even fashion. Its portrayal ranges from serious and ominous to satirical and playful. This theory resonates with those who feel distrustful of powerful institutions and seek simple explanations for complex global phenomena.

The Reality

The historical Illuminati was a short-lived organization with limited influence. The modern portrayal of the Illuminati as a secretive global power is a fabrication that capitalizes on the fears and uncertainties of modern society. While powerful entities and individuals do shape world events, the idea of a singular, all-controlling Illuminati remains within the realm of fiction.

4: Area 51 and the Aliens Among Us

For decades, Area 51 has been at the heart of conspiracy theories surrounding extraterrestrial life and government secrecy. Located in the Nevada desert, this highly classified U.S. Air Force facility is believed by many to be the site where alien technology and beings are studied and stored.

The Origins of the Theory

The mystery surrounding Area 51 began in the 1950s when the U.S. government started using the site for the testing of secretive military aircraft, such as the U-2 spy plane. The remote location and stringent security measures fueled speculation about the nature of activities conducted there.

Interest in Area 51 surged in 1989 when Bob Lazar, a self-proclaimed former Area 51 employee, claimed in a television interview that he had worked on reverse-engineering alien technology at the site. Lazar's stories of flying saucers and extraterrestrial beings sparked widespread fascination and skepticism.

Key Arguments and Counterarguments

1. **Alien Technology and Craft**
   o **Claim:** Area 51 is home to crashed alien spacecraft and advanced technologies recovered from these crafts, which the government has been secretly studying and reverse-engineering.
   o **Counter:** The U.S. government has consistently denied any involvement with extraterrestrial technology at Area 51. While the facility is known for developing cutting-edge aircraft, there is no verifiable evidence of alien technology.
2. **Extraterrestrial Beings**
   o **Claim:** The facility allegedly houses extraterrestrial beings, either alive or deceased, from crashes such as the purported incident in Roswell, New Mexico, in 1947.
   o **Counter:** No credible evidence has been presented to support claims of extraterrestrial life at Area 51. The Roswell incident itself has been explained as a military balloon crash.
3. **Government Secrecy and Cover-Ups**
   o **Claim:** The extreme secrecy and restricted access to Area 51 are cited as proof of the government's efforts to hide evidence of extraterrestrial life.
   o **Counter:** The secrecy surrounding Area 51 is primarily due to its role in the development and testing of advanced military technology. The facility's security measures are standard for sensitive military installations.

Cultural Impact

Area 51 has become synonymous with UFOs and government conspiracies in popular culture. It has been featured in numerous movies, television shows, and books, often depicted as the epicenter of alien-related activities. The fascination with Area 51 reached a peak in 2019 with the viral "Storm Area 51" event, where millions expressed interest in uncovering the site's secrets.

The Reality

Area 51 is a legitimate military testing facility, and its activities are classified for national security reasons. While its association with extraterrestrial life makes for compelling stories, there is no substantive evidence to support claims of alien technology or beings at the site. The enduring mystery of Area 51 serves as a powerful reminder of how secrecy and speculation can fuel enduring conspiracy theories.

5: JFK Assassination: The Cover-Up

The assassination of President John F. Kennedy in 1963 remains one of the most scrutinized events in modern history. Despite the official conclusion that Lee Harvey Oswald acted alone, numerous theories suggest that the true circumstances of Kennedy's death were covered up.

The Origins of the Theory

The Warren Commission, established to investigate Kennedy's assassination, concluded in 1964 that Oswald was the sole perpetrator. However, the commission's findings were met with skepticism and criticism. Discrepancies in eyewitness accounts, questions about the forensic evidence, and the political climate of the time contributed to widespread doubt.

Over the years, various individuals and groups have proposed alternative theories, ranging from the involvement of the CIA and the Mafia to allegations of a broader governmental or international conspiracy. Books, films, and documentaries have explored these possibilities, each adding new layers to the mystery.

Key Arguments and Counterarguments

1. **Multiple Shooters**
   - **Claim:** Some witnesses reported hearing shots from directions other than the Texas School Book Depository, suggesting the presence of multiple shooters.
   - **Counter:** The majority of forensic evidence and investigations, including the House Select Committee on Assassinations, have supported the conclusion that all shots came from the depository where Oswald was positioned.
2. **Magic Bullet Theory**
   - **Claim:** The single-bullet theory, which posits that one bullet caused multiple wounds to Kennedy and Texas Governor John Connally, is implausible and suggests a second shooter.
   - **Counter:** Detailed analysis of the bullet's trajectory and the relative positions of Kennedy and Connally have provided credible explanations supporting the single-bullet theory.
3. **Oswald's Connections**
   - **Claim:** Oswald's connections to Soviet and Cuban operatives, and his prior activities, indicate he may have been part of a larger plot.
   - **Counter:** While Oswald had various international contacts, investigations have not uncovered evidence linking these contacts to a conspiracy to assassinate Kennedy.
4. **The Role of Government Agencies**
   - **Claim:** The CIA, FBI, or other government agencies were involved in or covered up the assassination to protect their interests or those of powerful individuals.
   - **Counter:** Multiple investigations, including the Warren Commission and subsequent inquiries, found no credible evidence of direct involvement by these agencies in the assassination.

Cultural Impact

The assassination of JFK has had a profound impact on American culture and politics. It has been the subject of countless books, films, and television programs, each exploring different aspects of the event and the myriad theories surrounding it. The persistent doubts and speculation reflect broader societal concerns about transparency and trust in government.

The Reality

While many questions about the JFK assassination remain, the most credible evidence supports the conclusion that Lee Harvey Oswald acted alone. The ongoing fascination with the event underscores the human desire to find meaning in tragedy and to question official narratives. The JFK assassination remains a powerful example of how uncertainty and complexity can give rise to enduring conspiracy theories.

6: Big Pharma and the Suppression of Cures

The pharmaceutical industry, often referred to as "Big Pharma," is a frequent target of conspiracy theories. These theories claim that pharmaceutical companies suppress cures for diseases to maintain their profits and control over the healthcare market.

The Origins of the Theory

The perception of Big Pharma as a profit-driven, powerful entity has long fueled skepticism and mistrust. This image has been reinforced by high-profile cases of unethical behavior, such as price gouging, marketing of harmful drugs, and withholding of critical research data. These actions have led to a belief that pharmaceutical companies prioritize profits over patient welfare.

The theory that Big Pharma suppresses cures is often linked to alternative medicine advocates and critics of the healthcare system. They argue that natural or inexpensive treatments are deliberately marginalized in favor of costly pharmaceuticals.

Key Arguments and Counterarguments

1. **Suppression of Natural Cures**
   - **Claim:** Pharmaceutical companies suppress or discredit natural remedies and alternative treatments to protect their market share.
   - **Counter:** While some natural treatments have merit, most pharmaceutical drugs undergo rigorous testing and regulation to ensure their safety and efficacy. The complexity and variability of natural remedies often make them difficult to standardize and test to the same degree.
2. **Withholding of Effective Treatments**
   - **Claim:** There are claims that effective cures for diseases like cancer exist but are suppressed by Big Pharma to continue profiting from ongoing treatments.
   - **Counter:** Medical research is a highly competitive and collaborative field. If a cure were discovered, it would be nearly impossible to keep it hidden due to the large number of researchers and institutions involved in medical science.
3. **Price Manipulation and Accessibility**
   - **Claim:** Big Pharma manipulates drug prices and patents to maximize profits, often at the expense of patient access to essential medications.
   - **Counter:** While there are legitimate concerns about drug pricing and access, these issues are often more complex and involve multiple factors, including research and development costs, regulatory policies, and healthcare infrastructure.
4. **Influence on Healthcare Policies**
   - **Claim:** Pharmaceutical companies have undue influence over healthcare policies and regulations, often resulting in policies that favor their interests over public health.
   - **Counter:** While the pharmaceutical industry does exert significant influence, it operates within a regulatory framework designed to balance public health needs with innovation and industry viability.

Cultural Impact

The image of Big Pharma as a malevolent force has been reinforced by media portrayals and publicized scandals. Films, books, and documentaries often depict pharmaceutical companies as profit-driven entities willing to go to great lengths to protect their interests. This perception fuels ongoing debates about the role of these companies in healthcare and the need for regulatory oversight.

The Reality

The pharmaceutical industry plays a critical role in developing and providing treatments for a wide range of medical conditions. While it is true that the industry has been involved in unethical practices and faces significant challenges related to pricing and access, the idea that it suppresses cures for diseases is unsupported by credible evidence. Addressing the legitimate concerns about Big Pharma requires nuanced understanding and policy solutions rather than conspiracy theories.

7: The New World Order

The New World Order (NWO) is a broad conspiracy theory that suggests a secretive global elite is working to establish a totalitarian world government. Proponents believe that this elite manipulates political and economic systems to consolidate power and control over the world's population.

The Origins of the Theory

The concept of a New World Order has historical roots in fears of centralized power and authoritarianism. The term gained prominence in the 20th century, particularly after World War II and during the Cold War, when concerns about global governance and international organizations became prevalent.

The modern iteration of the New World Order theory often incorporates elements from various other conspiracy theories, including those involving the Illuminati, Freemasonry, and secretive government operations. It suggests that events such as economic crises, wars, and political upheavals are orchestrated to advance the agenda of this shadowy group.

Key Arguments and Counterarguments

1. **Global Organizations and Centralized Power**
   - **Claim:** International organizations like the United Nations, the World Bank, and the International Monetary Fund are tools used by the NWO to consolidate power and control global affairs.
   - **Counter:** These organizations are composed of member states with varying interests and agendas. While they wield significant influence, their actions are subject to scrutiny and accountability from a diverse range of stakeholders.
2. **Economic and Financial Control**
   - **Claim:** The NWO manipulates global financial systems to create economic crises and gain control over nations through debt and financial dependency.
   - **Counter:** Economic crises are complex phenomena influenced by numerous factors, including policy decisions, market dynamics, and geopolitical events. The idea of a single entity orchestrating these crises oversimplifies these complexities.
3. **Surveillance and Control**
   - **Claim:** Advances in technology, particularly in surveillance and data collection, are tools used by the NWO to monitor and control the global population.
   - **Counter:** While concerns about privacy and surveillance are legitimate, these technologies are developed and used by a wide range of actors, including governments, corporations, and individuals. The regulation and oversight of these technologies are critical issues that require public discourse and legal frameworks.
4. **Military and Political Manipulation**
   - **Claim:** Wars, political upheavals, and regime changes are orchestrated by the NWO to destabilize regions and establish control.

- o **Counter:** Conflicts and political changes often result from a combination of internal and external factors, including local grievances, power struggles, and international interests. While external influences can play a role, attributing these events to a single controlling entity is reductive.

Cultural Impact

The New World Order theory has influenced a wide range of cultural and political discourses. It has been referenced in literature, films, and political rhetoric, often as a symbol of the dangers of unchecked power and globalism. The theory resonates with individuals who are skeptical of globalization and fear the loss of national sovereignty and individual freedoms.

The Reality

The concept of a New World Order as an all-encompassing global conspiracy lacks credible evidence and is largely speculative. While concerns about the concentration of power and the role of international organizations are valid, they do not support the existence of a coordinated plot to establish a totalitarian world government. Understanding and addressing the challenges of global governance and power dynamics requires a grounded approach rooted in facts and analysis.

8: Chemtrails: The Secret Government Experiments

The chemtrail conspiracy theory suggests that the trails left by aircraft are not merely water vapor but chemical or biological agents deliberately sprayed into the atmosphere by governments or other entities for undisclosed purposes.

The Origins of the Theory

The theory emerged in the late 1990s and early 2000s, coinciding with increased visibility of contrails from high-altitude aircraft. Proponents argue that these trails are part of a secret program involving weather modification, population control, or other nefarious activities.

This belief is often linked to broader suspicions about government secrecy and technological manipulation. The theory has been popularized through various online communities, documentaries, and public figures who claim to have insider knowledge or observational evidence of chemtrails.

Key Arguments and Counterarguments

1. **Unusual Patterns and Persistence**
   - **Claim:** Chemtrails exhibit unusual patterns and persist longer than typical contrails, indicating they are composed of substances other than water vapor.
   - **Counter:** The persistence and appearance of contrails are influenced by atmospheric conditions, such as temperature, humidity, and wind. Scientists have extensively studied contrails and found no evidence that they contain anything other than ice crystals formed from aircraft exhaust.
2. **Health and Environmental Effects**
   - **Claim:** Chemtrails are responsible for a variety of health issues, environmental damage, and changes in weather patterns.
   - **Counter:** No scientific studies have validated these claims. Air quality monitoring and environmental studies have found no harmful substances or patterns consistent with the chemtrail theory. Health and environmental effects attributed to chemtrails are often explainable by other, more conventional causes.
3. **Government Secrecy and Intentions**
   - **Claim:** Governments are conducting secret experiments or operations involving chemtrails for purposes such as geoengineering, population control, or testing biological agents.
   - **Counter:** While there are ongoing discussions and research about geoengineering, these activities are conducted openly and with regulatory oversight. The idea of covert large-scale spraying operations lacks credible evidence and would be nearly impossible to carry out without public detection and whistleblowing.
4. **Visual and Anecdotal Evidence**
   - **Claim:** Observations of unusual aircraft behavior and personal anecdotes provide evidence of chemtrail operations.
   - **Counter:** Visual and anecdotal evidence is highly subjective and often misinterpreted. The behavior of aircraft and the appearance of contrails can be explained by normal flight operations and atmospheric science.

Cultural Impact

The chemtrail theory has gained a significant following, with dedicated online communities and activists advocating for public awareness and government transparency. It has been featured in various media, often as part of broader narratives about government secrecy and environmental concerns.

The Reality

The scientific consensus is that contrails are a natural byproduct of aircraft engines operating at high altitudes and are composed of water vapor and ice crystals. The persistence and appearance of these trails are determined by atmospheric conditions. The chemtrail theory lacks credible evidence and is largely dismissed by experts in aviation and atmospheric science. Efforts to address environmental and health concerns should focus on well-documented issues rather than speculative and unverified claims.

9: Flat Earth Theory: A Misguided Belief

The Flat Earth theory posits that the Earth is not a globe but a flat, disc-shaped object. This belief, which contradicts centuries of scientific evidence and exploration, has seen a resurgence in recent years, driven by online communities and social media.

The Origins of the Theory

Flat Earth beliefs have existed in various forms throughout history. Ancient cultures had diverse cosmological models, some of which depicted a flat Earth. However, the concept was largely debunked and replaced by the understanding of a spherical Earth as early as the ancient Greek period, with further validation from observations, scientific advancements, and space exploration.

The modern Flat Earth movement gained traction in the 19th century with figures like Samuel Rowbotham, who published works arguing against the spherical model. In recent years, the theory has been revitalized through online platforms, where proponents share their interpretations and challenge mainstream science.

Key Arguments and Counterarguments

1. **Visual Perception and Horizon**
   - **Claim:** Observers see a flat horizon and no curvature, suggesting the Earth is flat.
   - **Counter:** The curvature of the Earth is subtle and not easily observable at ground level. High-altitude photography and observations from space clearly show the Earth's curvature. The appearance of a flat horizon is a result of the Earth's vast size relative to the observer's vantage point.
2. **Lack of Direct Evidence for a Globe**
   - **Claim:** Flat Earthers argue that the evidence for a spherical Earth is indirect or manipulated and that personal observations suggest a flat surface.
   - **Counter:** Numerous lines of evidence, including satellite imagery, global navigation systems, and the physics of gravity, support the spherical model of the Earth. The consistency and reproducibility of these observations across different methods and technologies confirm the Earth's shape.
3. **Misinterpretation of Scientific Principles**
   - **Claim:** Flat Earth proponents often misinterpret or reject principles of physics, such as gravity and the behavior of water, to argue for a flat Earth.
   - **Counter:** Scientific principles are based on empirical evidence and consistent observations. Gravity explains the spherical shape of celestial bodies and the behavior of objects on Earth's surface. Misinterpretations arise from a lack of understanding of these concepts.
4. **Conspiracy and Misinformation**
   - **Claim:** The belief in a spherical Earth is a conspiracy perpetuated by governments, space agencies, and scientists to hide the truth.

- ○ **Counter:** The idea of a global conspiracy to promote the spherical Earth model is implausible. The overwhelming consensus among scientists and the corroborating evidence from independent sources worldwide debunk the notion of such a coordinated effort.

Cultural Impact

The resurgence of the Flat Earth theory reflects broader themes of skepticism towards scientific authority and institutional trust. It highlights the challenges of misinformation in the digital age, where individuals can easily find and share content that aligns with their beliefs. The Flat Earth movement has generated significant media attention and debate, often serving as a case study in the spread of pseudoscience.

The Reality

The Earth is unequivocally spherical, as confirmed by centuries of scientific inquiry and exploration. The persistence of Flat Earth beliefs underscores the importance of scientific literacy and critical thinking in evaluating information. While the theory provides a fascinating look at human psychology and the power of community, it remains fundamentally flawed and unsupported by credible evidence.

10: The Bermuda Triangle

The Bermuda Triangle, also known as the "Devil's Triangle," is a region in the western part of the North Atlantic Ocean where numerous ships and aircraft are said to have disappeared under mysterious circumstances. This area, roughly bounded by Miami, Bermuda, and Puerto Rico, has been the subject of speculation and intrigue for decades.

The Origins of the Theory

The legend of the Bermuda Triangle began to take shape in the mid-20th century, with reports of unexplained disappearances and strange phenomena dating back to the early 1900s. The term "Bermuda Triangle" was coined by writer Vincent Gaddis in a 1964 article, where he described the area as a "graveyard of ships and planes."

Subsequent authors and researchers expanded on Gaddis's work, weaving together stories of vanished vessels, ghost ships, and unexplained anomalies. Theories about the causes of these disappearances range from natural explanations, like rogue waves and magnetic anomalies, to more fantastical ideas involving aliens, time warps, and underwater cities.

Key Arguments and Counterarguments

1. **Unexplained Disappearances**
   - **Claim:** The Bermuda Triangle is a hotspot for unexplained disappearances of ships and aircraft, far exceeding the number expected in other parts of the world.
   - **Counter:** Detailed analyses and statistical studies have shown that the number of incidents in the Bermuda Triangle is comparable to other heavily trafficked regions of the world. Many of the disappearances attributed to the Triangle can be explained by human error, weather conditions, and mechanical failures.
2. **Magnetic Anomalies**
   - **Claim:** The region is said to experience unusual magnetic anomalies that can disrupt navigation systems and lead to the loss of ships and planes.
   - **Counter:** While the Bermuda Triangle does have some areas of magnetic variation, these are not unique and are well-documented by navigational charts. Modern navigation systems are designed to account for such variations, reducing the risk of disorientation.
3. **Rogue Waves and Weather Phenomena**
   - **Claim:** Sudden and powerful rogue waves, waterspouts, and storms in the Bermuda Triangle can cause vessels to sink without a trace.
   - **Counter:** The North Atlantic is known for its volatile weather and sea conditions, which can indeed be dangerous for maritime and air travel. However, these phenomena are natural and occur in many parts of the world, not just the Bermuda Triangle.
4. **Extraterrestrial and Paranormal Theories**
   - **Claim:** Some theories propose that the Bermuda Triangle is a site of alien activity, underwater bases, or time warps that account for the mysterious disappearances.
   - **Counter:** These theories lack credible evidence and are often based on anecdotal accounts and speculative interpretations. The majority of disappearances can be explained by conventional causes.

Cultural Impact

The Bermuda Triangle has become a cultural phenomenon, inspiring countless books, movies, and documentaries. Its reputation as a mysterious and dangerous place has captured the public's imagination, making it a popular topic for exploration and adventure stories. The Triangle's allure lies in its combination of real-world danger and speculative mystery.

The Reality

The Bermuda Triangle is a heavily traveled region of the ocean with a history of accidents and incidents, much like any other busy maritime area. While its reputation for mystery is compelling, the majority of disappearances can be explained by natural causes and human factors. The enduring fascination with the Bermuda Triangle highlights our tendency to seek out the extraordinary in the face of the unknown.

11: Mind Control and MK-Ultra

The idea of government mind control programs has long been a staple of conspiracy theories, often centered around the CIA's MK-Ultra project. This secretive program, conducted during the Cold War, involved experiments on unwitting individuals to explore the possibilities of mind control, brainwashing, and psychological manipulation.

The Origins of the Theory

MK-Ultra was a real program initiated by the CIA in the early 1950s. It aimed to investigate the use of drugs, hypnosis, and other techniques for interrogations and psychological warfare. The program included experiments on human subjects, often without their consent, and used a variety of methods, including the administration of LSD and other substances.

The existence of MK-Ultra was officially acknowledged in the 1970s, leading to congressional hearings and public outrage. The revelations about the program fueled numerous conspiracy theories about ongoing government mind control efforts and the extent of MK-Ultra's activities.

Key Arguments and Counterarguments

1. **Scope and Impact of MK-Ultra**
   - **Claim:** MK-Ultra involved widespread and inhumane experiments on civilians and military personnel, many of which remain undisclosed.
   - **Counter:** While MK-Ultra's scope and ethical violations were significant, much of what is known about the program has been documented through declassified files and testimonies. The full extent of the program's impact is difficult to assess due to the destruction of many records, but extensive investigations have uncovered key details.
2. **Ongoing Mind Control Programs**
   - **Claim:** Government mind control experiments did not end with MK-Ultra and continue in secret under different names and guises.
   - **Counter:** There is no credible evidence to support the existence of ongoing government mind control programs on the scale of MK-Ultra. Modern ethical standards and oversight make it unlikely that such programs could operate undetected in contemporary society.
3. **Manipulation Through Media and Technology**
   - **Claim:** Governments and corporations use media, technology, and psychological techniques to manipulate and control public perception and behavior.
   - **Counter:** While media and technology can influence public opinion and behavior, this influence is not equivalent to the direct mind control envisioned in MK-Ultra. Public awareness and media literacy are critical in understanding and mitigating these influences.
4. **Victim Accounts and Anecdotal Evidence**
   - **Claim:** Individuals claiming to be victims of mind control experiments provide firsthand evidence of ongoing programs.

- o **Counter:** Personal accounts can be compelling, but they often lack verifiable evidence and can be influenced by psychological and sociocultural factors. Thorough investigation and corroboration are necessary to substantiate such claims.

Cultural Impact

MK-Ultra has had a profound impact on public consciousness, fueling numerous books, movies, and conspiracy theories about mind control and government overreach. It has become a symbol of the dangers of unchecked government power and the ethical boundaries of scientific research. The program's legacy continues to influence debates about privacy, surveillance, and the limits of governmental authority.

The Reality

MK-Ultra was a real and ethically troubling program that involved significant violations of human rights. The revelations about its activities have led to greater scrutiny of government actions and the establishment of ethical guidelines for research. While the idea of ongoing mind control programs remains a topic of speculation, there is no substantive evidence to support such claims beyond the documented history of MK-Ultra. Understanding the program's history helps us grapple with the ethical implications of scientific and governmental power.

12: The Truth About the Covid-19 Pandemic

The Covid-19 pandemic, which began in late 2019, has been accompanied by a surge in conspiracy theories about its origins, spread, and the responses to it. These theories have ranged from allegations of the virus being a bioweapon to claims about global control agendas orchestrated by powerful elites.

The Origins of the Theory

The rapid spread and severe impact of Covid-19, combined with the unprecedented global response, created fertile ground for conspiracy theories. Early uncertainty about the virus's origin, conflicting information from health authorities, and the implementation of strict public health measures contributed to widespread speculation and mistrust.

Conspiracy theories about Covid-19 often center around its origin, the role of governments and pharmaceutical companies, and the measures taken to control its spread. These theories have been propagated through social media, online forums, and public figures, creating significant challenges for public health communication and policy.

Key Arguments and Counterarguments

1. **Laboratory Origin**
   - **Claim:** The virus was deliberately created or accidentally released from a laboratory, such as the Wuhan Institute of Virology.
   - **Counter:** Scientific investigations suggest that the virus is of natural origin, likely emerging from a zoonotic source. While the exact pathway of transmission to humans is still under study, there is no conclusive evidence supporting the lab origin theory. Numerous scientific studies and international investigations support the natural origins of the virus.
2. **Bioweapon Claims**
   - **Claim:** Covid-19 is a bioweapon intentionally released to cause global disruption and achieve geopolitical or economic goals.
   - **Counter:** There is no credible evidence to support the claim that Covid-19 is a bioweapon. The genetic structure of the virus shows no signs of human manipulation, and its spread and impact are consistent with a naturally occurring infectious disease.
3. **Government Control and Surveillance**
   - **Claim:** Governments are using the pandemic as a pretext to impose draconian measures, increase surveillance, and erode civil liberties.
   - **Counter:** While public health measures such as lockdowns and surveillance have raised legitimate concerns about privacy and freedom, these measures are generally aimed at controlling the spread of the virus and protecting public health. The balance between public safety and individual rights is a critical ongoing discussion.
4. **Vaccines and Population Control**
   - **Claim:** Covid-19 vaccines are part of a larger agenda to control or harm the population, including theories about microchips and sterilization.
   - **Counter:** Covid-19 vaccines have undergone rigorous testing and regulatory review to ensure their safety and efficacy. The claims about harmful effects and population control

are unsupported by scientific evidence and have been debunked by health authorities and experts worldwide.

Cultural Impact

The Covid-19 pandemic and the accompanying conspiracy theories have had a profound impact on society. They have influenced public attitudes towards health measures, vaccines, and government policies. The spread of misinformation has complicated efforts to manage the pandemic and highlighted the challenges of communicating scientific information in a polarized and rapidly changing environment.

The Reality

Covid-19 is a novel coronavirus that has caused a global health crisis. The scientific community continues to study its origins, transmission, and impact. While the pandemic has prompted significant social and political changes, the conspiracy theories surrounding it are largely unfounded and distract from the critical efforts to understand and combat the virus. Public health responses should be guided by credible scientific evidence and a commitment to transparency and public engagement.

13: The Deep State: Hidden Government Powers

The concept of the "Deep State" refers to a hidden network of power within the government that operates independently of elected officials and seeks to influence or control policy and decision-making. This theory suggests that a group of entrenched bureaucrats, intelligence agencies, and powerful elites work behind the scenes to shape the direction of the country.

The Origins of the Theory

The term "Deep State" originated in Turkey, where it was used to describe a clandestine network of military and intelligence officials who allegedly influenced government decisions. In the United States, the concept gained popularity in the 21st century, particularly in discussions about the influence of intelligence agencies and long-serving bureaucrats on national policy.

Proponents of the Deep State theory argue that this network operates across political administrations, pursuing its own agenda regardless of the will of the electorate. They point to actions by intelligence agencies, leaks of classified information, and resistance to certain policies as evidence of Deep State activity.

Key Arguments and Counterarguments

1. **Intelligence Agencies and Secrecy**
   - **Claim:** Intelligence agencies like the CIA and NSA operate with significant autonomy and influence, often pursuing their own agendas and resisting oversight.
   - **Counter:** While intelligence agencies do have a degree of operational independence, they are subject to oversight by elected officials and judicial review. Their actions are driven by national security priorities and legal mandates, not hidden agendas.
2. **Bureaucratic Resistance**
   - **Claim:** Career bureaucrats within government agencies undermine or resist policies that conflict with their interests or beliefs, effectively acting as a shadow government.
   - **Counter:** Bureaucratic inertia and internal disagreement are common in large organizations, including governments. These dynamics do not necessarily indicate a coordinated effort to subvert elected officials' policies.
3. **Elite Influence and Corruption**
   - **Claim:** Powerful elites, including wealthy individuals and corporations, exert undue influence over government decisions, often at the expense of public interests.
   - **Counter:** While there are legitimate concerns about the influence of money and lobbying in politics, these issues are part of broader democratic and regulatory challenges. Addressing them requires transparency and reform, not assumptions of a hidden, monolithic Deep State.
4. **Public Perception and Mistrust**
   - **Claim:** The Deep State operates in secrecy and manipulates public perception through control of information and media.

- **Counter:** Media and information landscapes are complex and influenced by various factors, including corporate interests, political agendas, and public demand. The idea of a single, coordinated entity controlling public perception oversimplifies these dynamics.

Cultural Impact

The Deep State theory has become a powerful narrative in political discourse, often used to explain or justify resistance to certain policies or officials. It has been invoked across the political spectrum, sometimes as a critique of entrenched power and sometimes as a defense against perceived interference.

The Reality

The concept of the Deep State captures real concerns about the influence of entrenched interests and the complexity of government operations. However, the theory often overstates the coherence and coordination of these influences, attributing to conspiracy what is more likely the result of bureaucratic processes, political disagreements, and the challenges of governance. Addressing these concerns requires robust democratic institutions, accountability, and public engagement.

Conclusion: Deciphering Fact from Fiction

Conspiracy theories provide a window into the human psyche, reflecting our fears, desires, and need for understanding in a complex world. They challenge us to question authority and seek truth, but they also risk leading us down paths of misinformation and mistrust.

Understanding the Appeal

Conspiracy theories often arise in times of crisis and uncertainty. They offer simple explanations for complex events, providing a sense of order and control. For some, they fulfill a psychological need to find meaning and connection in a chaotic world. The sense of community and identity formed around these beliefs can be powerful and enduring.

The Role of Media and Technology

The digital age has transformed the way conspiracy theories are created and disseminated. Social media platforms amplify these narratives, allowing them to reach vast audiences rapidly. The challenge of distinguishing credible information from misinformation is greater than ever, requiring critical thinking and media literacy.

The Impact on Society

Belief in conspiracy theories can have significant social and political consequences. They can undermine trust in institutions, fuel division, and distract from addressing real issues. At their worst, they can lead to violence and harm. Understanding the roots and dynamics of these beliefs is crucial in mitigating their negative effects.

Navigating the Landscape of Conspiracy Theories

In a world where information is abundant and often conflicting, how do we navigate the landscape of conspiracy theories?

1. **Critical Thinking:** Develop the ability to evaluate information critically, considering the source, evidence, and context.
2. **Media Literacy:** Understand how media shapes and presents information, and learn to recognize bias and manipulation.
3. **Open Dialogue:** Engage in open and respectful discussions with others, even when their views differ, to broaden understanding and reduce polarization.
4. **Seek Evidence:** Prioritize evidence-based information and be willing to revise beliefs in light of new, credible evidence.
5. **Support Transparency:** Advocate for transparency and accountability in institutions to build trust and reduce the appeal of conspiratorial thinking.

Moving Forward

Conspiracy theories will likely always be a part of human culture, reflecting our quest for understanding and our suspicion of hidden forces. By approaching them with a balance of skepticism and openness, we can better navigate their complexities and focus on building a more informed and resilient society.

In the end, the journey through the world of conspiracy theories is a journey through our own minds and societies. It challenges us to think critically, engage empathetically, and seek truth in a world that is often stranger and more fascinating than fiction.

Tin Foil Hat and Technology: A Modern Fusion

As technology advances, so too can the designs and functionality of your tin foil hats. Here are some ways to integrate modern tech into your hat-making endeavors:

1. **LED Lighting:** Incorporate LED lights into your hat for a futuristic look and added visibility at night. Battery-powered strips or individual lights can be attached to highlight your hat's features.
2. **Smart Features:** Experiment with adding smart technology to your hat, such as sensors that detect electromagnetic fields or Bluetooth speakers for a musical touch. These additions can turn your hat into a multifunctional piece of wearable tech.
3. **3D Printing:** Use 3D printing to create custom components or embellishments for your tin foil hat. This technology allows for precise and intricate designs that can enhance both the aesthetics and functionality of your hat.
4. **Augmented Reality (AR) Integration:** Combine your hat with AR technology to create interactive experiences. For example, wear your hat while using an AR app that overlays digital information about electromagnetic fields or signal sources in your environment.

The Philosophy Behind the Hat

Wearing a tin foil hat can also be a philosophical statement. It represents a stance on individualism, skepticism, and the quest for truth. Here's how to embrace the deeper meaning behind your headgear:

1. **Symbol of Individualism:** Your tin foil hat is a declaration of your unique perspective and individuality. It says, "I think for myself, and I'm not afraid to stand out." Embrace this symbol as a reminder to always stay true to your beliefs and values.
2. **Championing Skepticism:** In a world filled with information and misinformation, your hat serves as a beacon of skepticism. It encourages you to question what you hear and see, to seek evidence, and to make informed decisions.
3. **Pursuit of Knowledge:** The hat is also a symbol of the pursuit of knowledge. It reflects a desire to understand and protect oneself against the unknown. Wear it as a badge of your commitment to learning and exploring the mysteries of life.
4. **Balance Between Belief and Humor:** The tin foil hat lifestyle strikes a balance between genuine belief and playful humor. It's about taking serious subjects with a pinch of salt and finding joy in the eccentric. Let this balance guide your approach to life's complexities.

Future of Tin Foil Hats

What does the future hold for tin foil hats? As we continue to explore new frontiers in science, technology, and culture, the role of the tin foil hat will evolve. Here's a glimpse into what might be next:

1. **New Materials and Designs:** Advances in materials science could lead to the development of more effective and stylish tin foil hats. Imagine hats made from lightweight composites or with integrated nanotechnology for superior signal blocking.
2. **Cultural Shifts:** As society's relationship with technology and surveillance changes, so too might the symbolism of the tin foil hat. It could become a mainstream fashion statement or a tool for digital privacy in an increasingly connected world.

3. **Global Movements:** The tin foil hat could inspire global movements that advocate for transparency, privacy, and the right to mental autonomy. As awareness grows, the hat may become a unifying symbol for those seeking to protect their minds and rights.
4. **Integration with Wearable Tech:** As wearable technology becomes more prevalent, the tin foil hat might evolve into a high-tech accessory that combines style, protection, and functionality. It could be the next frontier in the fusion of fashion and technology.

Living the Tin Foil Hat Lifestyle

Ultimately, living the tin foil hat lifestyle is about more than just wearing a shiny hat. It's about embracing curiosity, creativity, and a playful approach to the mysteries of life. Here's how to fully integrate this mindset into your everyday existence:

- **Stay Informed:** Keep learning about the world around you. Whether it's the latest in electromagnetic research or new crafting techniques, staying informed helps you make the most of your tin foil hat.
- **Question and Explore:** Don't be afraid to question the status quo and explore new ideas. Your tin foil hat is a symbol of your willingness to think outside the box and seek out unconventional solutions.
- **Share and Connect:** Share your passion for tin foil hats with others. Connect with like-minded individuals, engage in discussions, and contribute to the community's knowledge and creativity.
- **Have Fun:** Above all, remember to have fun. The tin foil hat lifestyle is about enjoying the journey, finding humor in the absurd, and celebrating the uniqueness of each individual.

FAQs

Will wearing a tin foil hat really protect me from mind control?

Absolutely! The tin foil hat acts as a shield against any unwanted, mind-controlling thoughts.   Plus, it adds a touch of style to your outfit!

Can I decorate my tin foil hat with glitter and stickers?

Of course! Let your creativity shine through your tin foil hat by adding glitter, stickers, or even a feather to make it uniquely yours. Just remember, the more bling, the better the protection!

How do I know if my tin foil hat is working?

If you suddenly find yourself free from any government surveillance or alien mind probes, then congratulations, your tin foil hat is doing its job! Keep rocking that stylish headgear.

Can I wear my tin foil hat in the shower?

While we admire your dedication to protection, we recommend keeping your tin foil hat dry. Save it for shielding your thoughts, not your hairdo!

What should I do if people laugh at my tin foil hat?

Embrace the haters! Remember, you're the trendsetter here. Let their laughter be your motivation to rock that tin foil hat with even more confidence.

And with that, you're ready to step out into the world, shining brightly under your custom-crafted, meticulously reinforced, and philosophically significant tin foil hat. Whether you're protecting your thoughts, making a fashion statement, or simply having fun, the journey with your tin foil hat is just beginning.

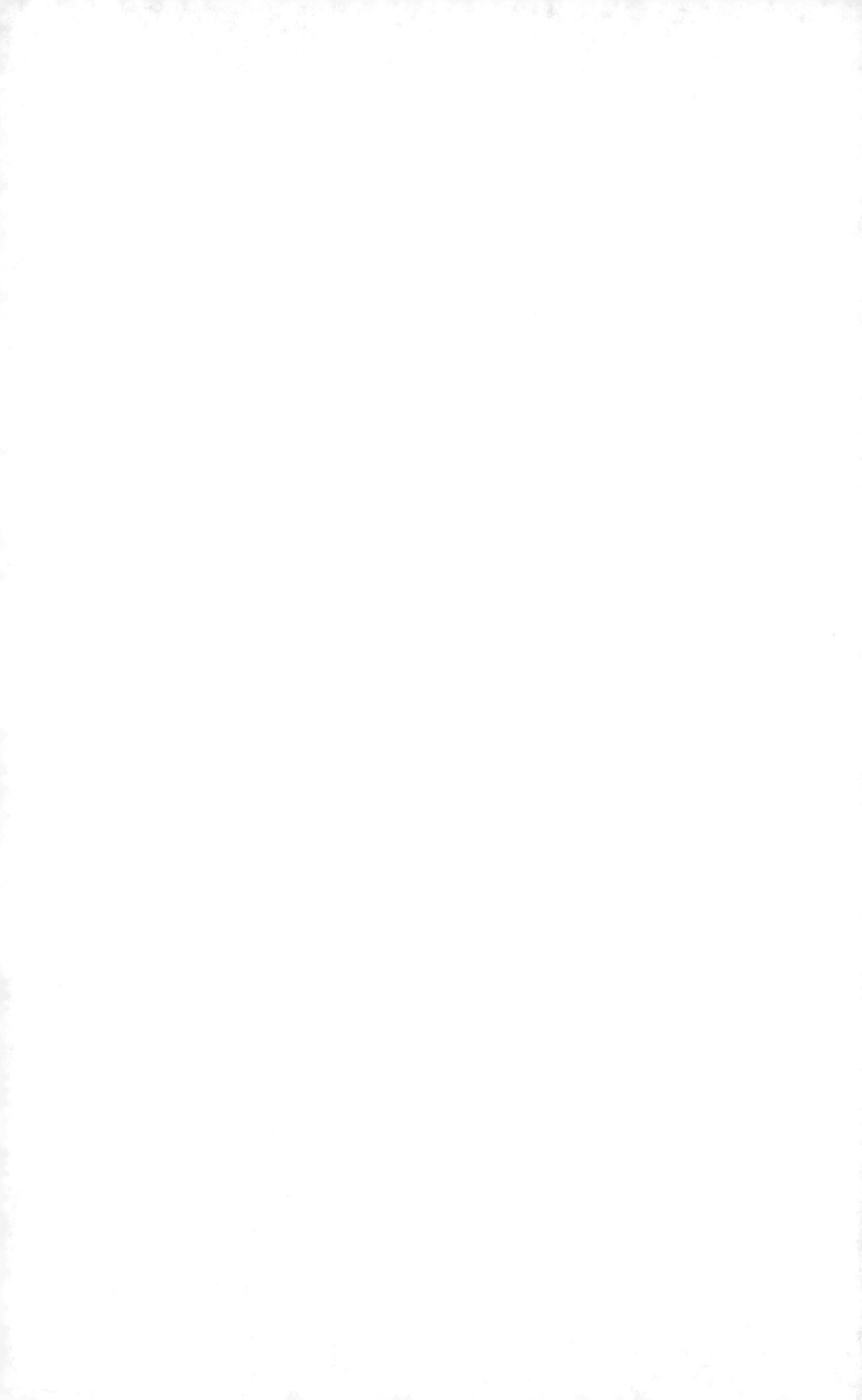

www.ingramcontent.com/pod-product-compliance
Lightning Source LLC
Chambersburg PA
CBHW072001210526
45479CB00003B/1019